To

Au

Fading Memories

of Coleraine, Portrush and Portstewart.

Printed by Impact Printing
Coleraine & Ballycastle

ISBN 0-948154-47-0

The publication of Fading Memories
has benefitted from the generous support
of

mᶜafee

PROPERTIES & MORTGAGES

Property Agents : Financial Services

Creating tomorrow's memories today.

FADING MEMORIES

20th Century images from the Coleraine area

Rapid change in the outward appearance of the streets in and around my home town, particularly during my own lifetime, has prompted me to gather together this interesting selection of images of how the town and its surroundings looked before and whilst I was growing up.

Many of the buildings illustrated have changed considerably, some have disappeared completely although the actual Coleraine town centre street pattern hasn't changed since it was laid out during the Plantation times of the 17th Century. Some of the smaller streets, however, have totally vanished while others have had major facelifts and are now barely recognisable. Long established and fondly remembered family businesses have disappeared from the town and new and brash multiples have arrived to take their place, sometimes occupying the same sites but sporting their modern corporate shopfronts and glitzy interiors.

Between 1981 and 1992 my friend and colleague Tommy McDonald and I produced a series of four books under the title of "Memories in Focus". These books, which proved very popular, illustrated the towns of the Triangle area as they appeared in earlier times, particularly during the late 19th and early 20th Centuries. This volume brings up to date many of the changes that have taken place in and around the Coleraine borough since then whilst also including an interesting selection of older images that have been discovered since the last volume of "Memories in Focus" was produced.

Included is a particularly comprehensive selection of images of the Killowen area taken in the late 1950s shortly before most of it was demolished in order to make way for new housing. These will probably generate great interest and I am particularly indebted to Mr. & Mrs. Noel Bigger for allowing me to use these excellent photographs taken by Mrs. Bigger's father, the late Mr. Robert Glassey.

As with the "Memories in Focus" series a work of this type would be an impossible task without the unselfish help and co-operation of a great number of other people. I wish to place on record my sincere thanks and appreciation to my wonderfully supportive wife Elizabeth and the following people in particular, without whose help this book would not have been possible :-

Jim Allen, Charlotte Anderson, Roy Anderson, Jim Cameron, Bobby Clyde, Jennifer Cunningham, Andy Houston, John Kennedy, Diane Kirkpatrick, Jacqueline McAlister, Sally McDonald, Tommy McDonald, Charlotte McKillop, Desmond Millar, Niall O'Boyle and Helen Perry (Museums Officer with Coleraine Borough Council for permitting access to, and use of, photos from the collection of the late Sammy Walker).

I hope that you enjoy this walk back in time through the streets that I grew up in and became familiar with when I was a small boy living in Brook Street. I feel fortunate to still be able to enjoy them today almost 60 years later.

Robert Anderson
October 2005

*This work is dedicated to the memory of
my late mother Susan who was happy to
spend her entire life as a resident of Coleraine.*

Church Street This postcard view from the early 1960s is a classic scene from the town at the time. The street is full of Morris, Austin, Rover and Standard cars as a message bike makes its way towards the Town Hall. Well known and long established local businesses line the street with Maypole, Moores, H. & T. Bellas and Tweedy Acheson prominent in this view.

The Diamond At first glance this seems to be a modern view of the western side of the Diamond. Look at it again however and it becomes apparent that this is a photograph from the 1970s. Still visible on the eerily empty streets are traffic markings and islands, the lack of traffic and people suggesting that this is in fact a Sunday afternoon. In the background premises then occupied by Hill Brothers, McGarvey's butchers and Paul Fashions are further clues as to the date.

Author's Collection

Diamond Shops In the previous photograph a new Northern Bank building stands on the corner of Queen Street and the Diamond. Prior to the new bank building the corner site was occupied by a range of local businesses including the Milk Bar, Christie's hardware store, Gilmour and Son jewellers shop and J. & D. Baxter's paint and wallpaper shop. Yet again the absence of people from the photo is unusual.

Author's Collection

Diamond Buses With bus stops clearly indicated by road markings and signage this 1961 view of the southern side of the Diamond presents a much livelier scene. People await buses here for Ballymoney, Kilrea, Bushmills, Limavady, Londonderry and Ballycastle. Evan Cox's tobacconist and Morelli's café did good business here at the time.

Author's Collection

Rooftop View This unusual view, taken from the roof of the Town Hall, dates from around the 1930s. The photo shows horse drawn carts and one lorry laden with flax at the regular flax market held here. In front of Tweedy Acheson's shop in Church Street is a group of farmers and merchants no doubt discussing the day's prices while an RUC officer makes his way up town.

Author's Collection

Post Office A Morris Minor car and an Austin pick-up truck are the only vehicles to be seen in this 1950s view of the Diamond. The Ulster Bank, Anderson's solicitors office, The Post Office and the Provincial Bank form the main element of the photo with some of the small houses in Bellhouse Lane visible on the right. Both the Post Office and Anderson's moved to New Row in later years.

Author's Collection

MacLarnon's Shop This newsagent and bookshop, needlework and toyshop was situated at the Town Hall end of the north side of Church Street. Pictured here in probably the late 1920s are the all female staff at the time. Many of the staff served the firm for many years and were again to be photographed outside a re-modelled shopfront in the 1930s. The contributor of this picture has both photos in his collection.

Courtesy Jim Allen

 Church Street Barely recognisable at first glance this view of Church Street and Kingsgate Street dates from the early 1930s. Taken from the roof of the Town Hall it illustrates well just how little traffic was around then. The pedestrianisation of the Town Centre and the addition of planters and trees is still a long way off and the town looks strangely empty some 70 years ago.

Courtesy Tommy McDonald

Disappearing Shops None of the shops illustrated in this mid 1960s view of Church Street are still trading today. The names of old established businesses such as Simpson & Hill, McCandless and Tweedy & Acheson are but a fading memory and how many can now recall Easiphit, Alf's, The Wimpy Bar and McCloskey's? As in the previous photo the absence of trees, now taken for granted in the pedestrian zone, is remarkable. The absence of people and traffic on the streets points to the photograph being taken on a Sunday afternoon or at a holiday period. *Author's Collection*

 Diamond Bomb The result of a huge van bomb explosion on 13th November 1992 is clearly evident in this photograph taken the morning after. Despite the bomb detonating just a few metres away the War Memorial of 1922 remained reasonably intact but the Town Hall and the landmark buildings surrounding it were severely damaged. Thankfully the area has been totally re-instated and today bears only a few minor scars of that terrible night.

Author's Collection

Queen Street This wonderful view of a snow covered Queen Street dates from around 1925. Few people are visible on the streets and only the tracks left by passing horse drawn carts and some footprints in the snow indicate a presence of people. In the background can be seen the Belfast Bank at the corner of Abbey Street and the business premises of D. Christie, Hydraulic and Sanitary Engineer and P. Kirby, Tinsmith can be noted in Queen Street.

Diane Kirkpatrick Collection

Morrison's Shop Mrs. Tilly Brown and Mr. J. C. Morrison pose outside his shop on Bridge Street in the early 1930s. This busy tobacconist and confectionery shop existed here under Morrison ownership from 1921 until 1971 when it passed to new owners. Mr. Morrison and his sons Ian and Robert, who ran the Railway Road shop, are still fondly remembered by natives of the town

Jennifer Cunningham Collection

Upper New Row Another street seldom photographed over the years comes under the attention here of Johnny Leonard, the local photographer. Most of the street looks similar today but vehicles and street signs give away the date as the 1950s. Not in existence today however are the small white painted houses on the right which seem to be of a very old style even then.

Author's Collection

Baptist Church The small church illustrated in this 1970s view of Abbey Street was the home of the Coleraine Baptist congregation from 1841 until 2002 when it was demolished to make way for a superb new building on the same historic site. It is believed that a Medieval settlement survived here prior to the Plantation in the 17th century and archaeological excavations at the time of the new church's construction tend to confirm this.

Author's Collection

Abbey Street Another traffic free, 1970s view of one of the town's more historic streets. Quite a number of the buildings illustrated here have undergone change and many are now awaiting redevelopment. The street was re-named from its original Meetinghouse Street at the end of the 19th century to reflect its proximity to the ancient St. Mary's Priory.

Society Street This little row of single storey dwellings existed in Society Street right up until the 1990s when the site was redeveloped. Most of the houses were occupied by pensioners and the redevelopment carried on that tradition. Society Street was named in honour of the Honourable the Irish Society who established the town through the Plantation of the 17th century.

Jacqueline McAlister Collection

Cross Lane Photographed here in the early 1970s prior to redevelopment this street was one of several that disappeared off the map of Coleraine. The area is now included within Abbey Street car park. Cross Lane, Stable Lane, Stone Row and Jail Street were lively communities complete with a pub, the Plough Inn, and several cafes in Stone Row.

Author's Collection

 Stable Lane Part of this street still survives today but barely recognisable when compared to this 1970s photo. On the right is the building housing the "Pals" club which had been in existence for the best part of 100 years. It later accommodated the fledgling Coleraine and District Motor Club. What appears to be a hanging basket is in fact a shrub growing out of the wall on the left.

Author's Collection

Ferryquay Street As its name implies this street led directly to a quay where at times, as a result of damage to or reconstruction of the bridge, a passenger ferry boat was operated across the river to Killowen. On the left stands Rothesay House variously used over the years as a home, clinic and council offices before being demolished in the 1980s to make way for the Rothesay Court complex.

Author's Collection

 Houses in Ferryquay Street Backing onto the gasworks these old and poor quality houses were photographed in the late 1950s by Robert Glassey and were fairly typical of the housing stock in Ferryquay Street then. Major redevelopment took place in the area and there is now very little evidence of where the street actually ran.

Bigger Collection

Coleraine Co-Operative Standing at the corner of Bridge Street and Hanover Place the Co-Op existed here for a number of years before moving to larger premises in Bridge Street. The Society was begun just after World War I by local railwaymen and finally closed in November 1966 having served the community for almost 50 years.

Courtesy Jim Allen

Watt's Coal Office Demolished during the development of the Dunnes Store complex at the Harbour this was the main office for the Watts coal business for over 100 years. Watts originally commenced business in Portrush in 1828, a fact noted on the stonework of their building, and later moved to Coleraine and became shipowners and coal importers. The firm was amalgamated into the Cawoods organisation in the 1980s.

Author's Collection

Tennis Courts This fine 1950s view of the tennis courts at Anderson Park on Millburn Road was taken from the railway embankment of the harbour branch line. In the background is the unmistakable skyline of Coleraine. Two fine rows of three storey houses are evident here in the shape of Harbourview Terrace, in the middle of the photo, and Castleview Terrace, since demolished, below and right of the Town Hall clock tower.

River Bann This snow scene was photographed before harbour development schemes made the photographer's vantage point inaccessible. A new quay was built here in 1956. The large trees in the background were in the grounds of the Manor House. Several still stand close to County Hall. On the right of the photo can be seen part of the old swing bridge that carried the railway line to Londonderry prior to 1924 when the new railway bridge was built to carry the line over the Bann.

Diane Kirkpatrick Collection

Millburn Road Railway Bridge A branch line to Coleraine Harbour was opened in 1892. At the time the main line to Londonderry crossed the Millburn Road at this point before a realignment of the track took place in 1923 taking in the new railway bridge over the Bann. The branch line continued to carry trains and wagons to the port until it was closed in 1963. This 1966 photograph clearly illustrates the old bridge before demolition and a number 139 double decker bus coming into town from Portrush.   *Maxwell Blair*

Clifton Terrace   Photographed around 1905 from the undeveloped waste land that became the Rose Gardens and Tennis Courts of Anderson Park the impressive Clifton Terrace stands next to Salem Lodge and another fine pair of Victorian semi-detached houses on Millburn Road. The terrace was named after the family of Lady Bruce of Downhill Castle.

Diane Kirkpatrick Collection

Bengers   A familiar sight since the 1930s to travellers and commuters from Portstewart and Portrush as they approached Coleraine was the red and cream brick structure of Benger's Milk Factory at Millburn. The tall brick chimney and distinctive factory architecture were as familiar to locals as the clock on the wall above the office entrance. The factory produced a variety of milk based products and had several name changes over the years including Bengers, Fisons, Pickerings and DPP Schreiber. The red brick structures were demolished in 2001.   *Author's Collection*

 Gasworks Situated at Hanover the gasworks dominated the riverside scene here from its inception in 1845 until its closure in the 1980s. Originally using coal imported to the nearby port the method of extracting gas remained virtually unchanged until the 1960s when oil based raw materials began to be used. Once the change over had taken place the tall retort building was demolished. The noise and smells from the gasworks are still well remembered.

Sammy Walker Collection courtesy Coleraine Borough Council

Bann Bridge and Clothworker's Building The bridge was built in 1844 and replaced an earlier structure on the same site. The large Clothworker's building was built shortly afterwards and for many years was known as the Clothworker's Hotel. In this photograph dating from the 1920s the building carries the logo "R. Douglas & Son Motor and Cycle Works". The tall chimney of Killowen Distillery can be seen in the background.   *Author's Collection*

Steam Crane This wonderful picture shows one of the first steam cranes to be employed at Coleraine Harbour and dates around 1900. The crane driver and another unidentified gent pose for the photographer with this state of the art machine. The engine builders can be identified as John H. Wilson of Sandhills, Liverpool from the name plate on the frame. Just behind the crane is one of the large buckets used to lift coal from ship's holds.

Author's Collection

The Harbour Many will remember fondly this familiar scene as photographed from the Bann Bridge. Several ships line the quay and are discharging timber and coal and loading pit props. The large number of local men finding employment discharging the loose timber from the German coaster ERICH HASLINGER can clearly be seen. The photo dates from October 1958.

Author's Collection

Awaiting Weather to Sail Another excellent example of just how busy the port once was is this February 1964 view of the harbour. The ships are all high in the water with derricks stowed indicating that they have been discharged and are awaiting calmer conditions at the Barmouth in order to sail. No fewer than seven ships are in port although one is hidden from view behind the others. The regular traders SILVERTHORN, BLACKTHORN and MAYTHORN are all here.

Author's Collection

Bridge Improvements Improvements to the road junction and footpaths are taking place in this early 1960s view of the Waterside end of the Bann Bridge. In the background a fine looking modern Dutch motorship discharges timber at the harbour's Number 1 Shed whilst the old steamship BANNPRIDE unloads general cargo into Number 2 Shed. This entire area of the port is now occupied by the modern Dunnes Store.

Author's Collection

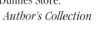

 Aerial Views These two pages are given over to sections of an aerial photograph of Coleraine taken about 1960. I have chosen two sections. There is a slight overlap to assist with location. In the first picture the points of interest are the Harbour, Union Street, Ballycastle Road and the still incomplete Harpur's Hill Estate as well as the Town Centre area.

Courtesy Jim Allen

Aerial Views The second picture takes in Bridge Street, Hanover, Waterside and Killowen areas and careful study illustrates just how much has been altered in the last 40 years.

Courtesy Jim Allen

Waterside This well composed shot of Waterside, as seen from the bottom of Captain Street, is another of the many surviving views taken by local photographer Johnny Leonard. Most impressive here are the trees on either side of the street and the telephone box on the left hand side is of a curious design. Yet again the presence of sunshine and an absence of heavy traffic give this 1950s shot an almost continental air.

Author's Collection

Strand Road By resting his camera on the wall along Strand Road the photographer has taken an unusual view of the road and its buildings. This dates again from the early 1950s and the building with the unusual roof line is the Harris Engineering Works that operated here for a number of years. On the right of the picture the area now known as Christie Park has yet to be developed and the river foreshore appears to be used as a dumping area.

Author's Collection

View to the West This fine panorama over Killowen was taken from the Mountsandel Road close to the old hospital site. A rather empty Strand Road is apparent and bare fields exist where the housing development of the "Heights" was built in later years. Clearly seen is the "new" Killowen Primary School, dating from 1936, and the Orange Hall which was previously the school. The picture dates from about 1940.

Courtesy Niall O'Boyle

Killowen Selection

The following pages contain a magnificent selection of photographs taken by the late Mr. Robert Glassey who was Deputy County Public Health Inspector for County Londonderry from 1949.

All the pictures were taken in March 1958 and illustrate the streets, buildings, houses and conditions to be found in this part of the borough at a time prior to the comprehensive redevelopments that took place a few years later. I personally remember the area like this even though I was only a 10 year old passing through on my way to visit relatives who lived in "The Heights".

The pictures simply begged to be published and I am extremely grateful to Mr. Glassey's daughter, Mrs. Margaret Bigger, and her husband Noel for allowing me permission to reproduce them here. They are an unequalled record of a period of time in a part of our town that has undergone massive change over the last 50 years.

I have let the pictures tell their own story and only add location, house numbers and people's names where appropriate. The people who were born, raised and who spent their lives in the area will surely be well able to recount their own memories.

 Number 2 Killowen Street with a magnificent Jaguar Mark II parked outside. Resplendent in whitewall tyres this desireable collector's vehicle also sports a local number plate. This plot is now the site of a well-presented Council flower garden.

This scrap yard existed here for generations and the picture illustrates a wide variety of bits and pieces from lorry cabs to baths that have been discarded. In the background are Dunlop's barber shop and Mullan's grocers shop.

The "Big Well Brae" from Strand Road enters Killowen Street on the left here beside McFeeley's clothes shop and further along the street is Herald's Fish and Chip shop next door to their grocery shop.

On the corner of Pate's Lane and Killowen Street was Wall's grocers shop.

Just a few yards further along Killowen Street on the corner of Dunlop Street was Vaul's sweet shop. The open space further down the street was the play park.

Still on Killowen Street the Elim Hall on the right of the picture was used for religious gatherings and meetings. The building was formerly Killowen Orange Hall. Behind it was an area known as the "Pool Yard".

The Killowen Bar owned by Jimmy Bradley, popularly known as "Cheerio", was another popular meeting place. Mr. Bradley is seen at the door of the pub chatting to local boys.

Numbers 64 to 68 Killowen Street. The old small pane sash windows upstairs on number 66 give some indication of the age of the property at the time of the photo. "Big Robert" McCandless stands at his front door at number 68.

Taken looking from Killowen Street this view includes house numbers 1 to 11 Pate's Lane.

Across the street and in shadow on the day of the photograph is the row containing numbers 2 to 48 Pate's Lane. Peacock, O'Hara and Miller families lived here.

 Killowen Street ends and Kyle's Brae begins. This photo shows the fronts of numbers 2 to 20 Kyle's Brae. This is where the Rankin and McGrath families lived amongst others.

The tiny nature of some of the houses in the area can be judged in this view of numbers 1 to 7 Kyle's Brae.

On the right hand side of the street on the steep climb towards Laurel Hill House stood the single storey dwellings indicated as numbers 25 to 51 Kyle's Brae. Another couple of present day classic cars in the form of an Austin van and a Triumph Herald are parked here.

Half way up Kyle's Brae on the left hand side were numbers 48 to 56.

 A marvellous shot of the row of single storey houses numbered 1 to 23 on Shuttle Hill. King's shop existed here and families Dysart, Gault and Johnston lived in the row.

Another gem illustrating numbers 34 to 40 Shuttle Hill with the roof of Killowen Orange Hall, formerly a school, visible in the background. A huge bag of coal sits outside number 38. The Hunter, Adams and McNabb families lived along here.

Smoke rises from the chimney of number 69 Kyle's Brae indicating that someone still lives in the property despite its rather dilapidated appearance.

Sitting on the steepest part of Kyle's Brae these houses at numbers 65 to 69 looked directly out at the large stone wall surrounding the Laurel Hill House estate.

Nurse's Home This is the Nurses' Home, an unremarkable building which stood adjacent to Bannview Hospital on the Mountsandel Road. No doubt it could tell its own stories though! The entire hospital site, with the exception of the listed "Workhouse" building dating from 1841, was cleared for new housing developments during 2003 following the opening of the new Causeway Hospital a short distance away.

Author's Collection

Loreto Convent Extensive modern school buildings now surround the original house dating from 1877 which was built as "Tiev Tara" for Hugh Anderson (of Anderson Park fame) and described in a newspaper article of the time as being "the most extensive and costly residence in the neighbourhood of Coleraine". This view dates from the early part of the 20th century and illustrates what was then called the Ursuline Convent and purchased after the death of Mr. Anderson. A girls' grammar school operated here until the 1980s when the school became co-educational.

Tommy McDonald Collection

The 'Irish Houses' These thatched dwellings on the outskirts of Coleraine were photographed in January 1962 shortly before they were demolished. The buildings, dating from the 18th century stood on a corner site just off the main Castlerock road close to the Wheatsheaf Road junction. At a time they were thought to be "out in the country" but urban sprawl now means that their site is within the town boundaries and close to major new developments.

Tommy McDonald Collection

Union Street There is evidence of "tampering" in this Victorian view as illustrated by the addition of several playful children in the middle of the road. Some of the people in the photo are real but the postcard manufacturers of the time tended to add interest to duller sections of the picture. The absence of any sort of traffic is remarkable on a main route to the railway station. Melbourne Terrace is situated on the left of the photo mid way along the street.

Jacqueline McAlister Collection

Adam's Place This little street disappeared when the tower block of Coleraine Technical College was built on the site in the 1970s. The street, situated off Brook Street, was renamed as George's Place following the Silver Jubilee of King George V, the reason for all the flags and bunting in this photo. Small communities such as this went to great lengths to decorate their street on such occasions in that more innocent age.

Sammy Walker Collection courtesy Coleraine Borough Council

Lynas's Fish Shop Situated on Brook Street close to the junction with Kingsgate Street this typical family owned shop traded for many years as the only supplier of fresh fish in the town. The Lynas family for a time had their own vessels working out of the fishing ports of County Down and later developed a successful frozen food business which still thrives in the town. *Author's Collection*

Boyd's Row This row of cottages stood on Long Commons at its junction with Chapel Square and just across the road from the present entrance into Long Commons car park. Originally thatched they were built by Robert Boyd of Coleraine Distillery and were presumably meant to house some of his workforce. Demolished in the late 1950s the site is currently occupied by Burke's sporting shop and a snooker club.

Bigger Collection

Adelaide Avenue This well composed photo dating from the late 1940s has Saint Malachy's Church at its centre and is a rare view of this street. Named after Adelaide Hay who owned the land it was built on, the street remains a popular, quiet residential area close to shops, schools and churches although these days it is slightly more difficult to find a car parking space!

Author's Collection

Society Street Only yards away from the bustle of Church Street this old building in Society Street was once used as the bandroom for the town's silver band. Demolished in the 1950s to make way for a new development of shops this photo was taken in September 1946. Society Street follows the original line of the 17th century eastern rampart of the Plantation town.

Author's Collection

Park Street In this view, taken by the author in the troubled year of 1972, the barrels across the end of the street highlight some of the traffic restrictions in force at the time. Formerly called Rosemary Lane the street was renamed in 1904 following the opening of the new town park. Demolished to make way for the Mall car park the street consisted mostly of small family homes many occupied by generations of the same family.

Author's Collection

Mall Housing
Well hidden from view from the town end of Park Street these two 1950s photos again show the poor quality of some of the occupied houses in the areas just off the main street and close to the Mall. This whole area was originally within the walled town.

Author's Collection

Park Street (Northern End) Another view of Park Street from the North Rampart and showing the opposite end of the street close to where the previous two pictures were taken. Even though this view dates from the early 1970s the absence of traffic is very apparent.

Sammy Walker Collection courtesy Coleraine Borough Council

Park Keeper's Cottage Demolished in 2003 this cottage stood for almost 100 years on Circular Road and was the residence for the full-time Park Keeper. The well tended lawns and flower beds were very much appreciated by the townsfolk. A novel feature seen here on the lawn, and probably never tampered with, is a weather station. Not far away is the park's own greenhouse.

Author's Collection

Brook and Swings Popular in my childhood and for many years before and after was the Brook that ran through the park. Small fish, eels and frogs attracted small boys to the area with their fishing nets and the swings proved popular with all ages.

Author's Collection

Lodge Road This uncluttered view of the Lodge Road taken from the Nursery Avenue junction gives a good impression of just how little vehicular traffic was around at the turn of the century. The Lodge Road was developed from about 1860 and contains many large Victorian properties of a mix of styles with well wooded and be-shrubbed gardens. Modern property developers have started to make an impact on the original sites.

Author's Collection

Masonic Hall This view of Lodge Road was taken in the 1920s. The Masonic Hall is the square building in the centre. The building on the left of the photograph was originally the Technical School before becoming the town's police station in the late 1920s. Nearby and closer to Kingsgate Street are the grandly named Alanbye Villas. Most of the large houses and terraces on Lodge Road were individually named by their builders.

Courtesy Niall O'Boyle

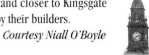

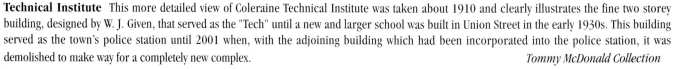

Technical Institute This more detailed view of Coleraine Technical Institute was taken about 1910 and clearly illustrates the fine two storey building, designed by W. J. Given, that served as the "Tech" until a new and larger school was built in Union Street in the early 1930s. This building served as the town's police station until 2001 when, with the adjoining building which had been incorporated into the police station, it was demolished to make way for a completely new complex.

Tommy McDonald Collection

Mill in Railway Road Photographed during the first phase of demolition in the mid 1970s this corn mill began life in the early 1800s and was originally powered by water from the brook that passes under Railway Road to this day. The mill suffered several fires during its lifetime and lay empty and derelict for many years. The entire area was redeveloped and the new property named Mill House reflecting its origins.

Sammy Walker Collection courtesy Coleraine Borough Council

Flour Mill This large mill existed on Railway Road until the early 1970s on a corner site occupied today by a car park. The mill was one of several in the area for which power was provided by the Brook and the Mill Dam. Coleraine Leisure Centre stands on the site of the Mill Dam and the Brook still flows under Railway Road. Millers, waggoners and a smartly dressed gent all appear in this photo which dates from around 1908.

Tommy McDonald Collection

Morrison and Cameron's Garage Situated in Railway Place off Railway Road from 1949 until 1970 this popular and busy garage was owned by local men Danny Cameron and Fergus Morrison. I recall Triumph cars being sold here and the tiny showroom window can be seen just to the right of the petrol pumps. Next door to the garage was the premises used by the Portrush and Coleraine Laundry Company who had their own boiler house providing steam and hot water. The tall chimney is visible in the photo.

John Kennedy Collection

Morrison's Café Across Railway Road from the laundry and garage Robert Morrison ran a small café, sweet shop and tobacconists opened by his father in the 1920s. The café was frequented by locals and travellers alike due to its proximity to the rail and bus stations and its popular owner was affectionately known to all as "Pop". The café was sold in 1968.

Jennifer Cunningham Collection

Railway Footbridge This bridge was provided by the Railway Company to allow pedestrian access across the lines when the gates were opened to allow the passage of trains to and from Portrush and Londonderry. The bridge was removed during the 1980s and later modifications were carried out to the crossing by removing the gates and adding automated barriers.

Sammy Walker Collection courtesy Coleraine Borough Council

Bushmills Road Not perhaps the most flattering of photographs this 1940s view of Bushmills Road taken from the railway crossing illustrates just how much the area has altered in the last sixty years. The amount of traffic on the road has certainly increased since then as a result of new industrial estates and many of the buildings on the right have been converted into commercial properties reflecting the additional residential areas at Millburn and Ballysally now served by the road.

Tommy McDonald Collection

Margueretta Terrace Situated on the Bushmills Road between James Street and Windsor Avenue this fine Victorian terrace is one of several on the road illustrated in this book for the first time. The corner grocer shop of J. Bethel also continued to operate under the ownership in more recent times of David Sloan and Shirlows before becoming the constituency offices for Gregory Campbell, M.L.A. and Member of Parliament for East Londonderry.

Jacqueline McAllister Collection

Olphert Place Directly across the Bushmills Road from Enfield Terrace and named after the Olphert family stands this row of houses again dating from the early part of the 20th Century. This row features fine bow windows to the properties. These are still used as family homes today. Some other family names existed in terrace names on Bushmills Road such as Coyle's Terrace and Flemingvale. These are difficult to locate today though.

Jacqueline McAlister Collection

New University A handwritten note on the back of the original of this photograph identifies it as being taken on Tuesday 18th April 1967. Seen here is Ginger Campbell laying the first bricks of what was to become the sprawling university complex on a green-field site just outside the town. In the background vehicles making deliveries of building materials include a rare three-wheeled Scammel truck belonging to local firm H. & T. Bellas.

Courtesy Niall O'Boyle

 McLernon's Standing on the roadside opposite the Salmon Leap the refreshment rooms operated by McLernon's provided visitors to the area with teas and coffee, mineral waters and chocolate whilst advertising "views of the leap". This was a popular, easy stroll away from the town and people visited the area to gaze at the river, Mountsandel opposite and the spectacle of Atlantic salmon jumping over the weir on their way upstream from the sea during the spawning period in early summer.

Diane Kirkpatrick Collection

Salmon Leap The exact date of this view is uncertain but is assumed to be about 1910. The photo illustrates the buildings that formed the Salmon Leap Public House and Coaching Inn beside the River Bann and on the main road to Kilrea at Castleroe. Substantially altered in later years the area is again to change considerably under recent development plans.

Diane Kirkpatrick Collection

Cummins' Steam Roller Henry Cummins owned a contracting business in Coleraine specialising in roadworks. Pictured here is one of his marvellous steam rollers known as "Progress" and sporting a fine nameplate in addition to its owner's plate. Today's road-building machine doesn't quite have the same charm or appeal of this beauty.

Diane Kirkpatrick Collection

Rural Pursuit A magnificent pair of Clydesdale horses are seen here in a ploughing competition outside Coleraine in the 1950s. The horses, Kate and Jane, are being worked by ploughman James Leighton of Bellemont as their owner James Young walks alongside. These wonderful animals were often among the prizewinners at ploughing matches in addition to earning their keep by working on the farms of their owners.

Courtesy Margaret McDonald

Delta All Stars Showband During the early 1960s and at the height of the showband era this group of talented local musicians formed the Delta All Stars Showband to perform at venues throughout the area. Seen in the photograph are, from left to right, John Beckett (drums), Brian McGrath (bass guitar), Sammy Kane (saxophone & clarinet), Johnny McBride (Manager), Bernie McDonald (vocals & trombone), Billy Mullan (guitar) and Mant Smith (accordion & clavoline).

Courtesy Niall O'Boyle

Causeway Tram This excellent shot of a rake of carriages of the famous "Giant's Causeway, Portrush and Bush Valley Railway and Tramway Company" was taken on the road between Bushmills and Portrush. The electrically driven engine number 22 is of the open "toast rack" type and is coupled up to an enclosed first class coach and another, covered, toast rack carriage. The tram operated from 1883 until 1949.

Diane Kirkpatrick Collection

Strand Road Junction Few would immediately recognise the junction of Strand Road and the Diamond in this 1960 view of Portstewart such are the alterations that have taken place since. The two storey block on the left of Strand Road was demolished in order to make the junction wider. At the time of the photo the property was vacant but had previously been occupied by McCurdy's cobblers shop. Next door was Deeney's confectionery and tobacconist shop and across the street was Shaw's tobacconist. Close examination of the picture reveals a little girl heading for her first communion accompanied by family and friends.

Courtesy Andrew Houston

Children's Bathing Place Another 1940s view highlights the fairly basic and unsophisticated facilities that were on offer to the holidaying family then and contrasts vividly with the same area today. In the background a banner on the Town Hall advertises a summer show by the Society Six Entertainers. No doubt these events were well patronised; after all there was no television!

Charlotte Anderson Collection

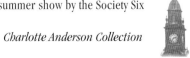

Doherty and Dunlop's Garage Mechanics and proprietor pose for the photographer at the door to Doherty and Dunlop's garage at the Diamond in Portstewart. These premises stood next door to the Anchor Bar and was the base for one of the early bus services in the area in addition to carrying out general motor repairs.

Author's Collection

Portstewart Hotels These two photographs illustrate well-known Portstewart hotels which have been demolished in recent years. On the right, dating from the 1950s is the Golf Hotel which was later sold, enlarged and rebranded to trade as the Edgewater Hotel. The picture on the left illustrates the nearby Strand Hotel about 1963. The Strand boasted a small outdoor swimming pool which in reality was little used. Both hotels commanded magnificent coastal views.

Tommy McDonald Collection

Portstewart Harbour Much has changed since this photograph was taken in the late 1940s. The majority of the buildings in the background here have either been demolished and rebuilt or are awaiting redevelopment. On the left the famous "Carrig-na-Cule" hotel has recently been reborn as a modern apartment block and McKinney's grocery shop, MacLarnon's tobacconist shop, the Medical Hall and the Windsor and Beach House Hotels have all suffered the ravages of time. Fishing nets set out to dry are reminders that this was once an active fishing port. *Charlotte Anderson Collection*

The "Violet Clarke" Taken during the 1950s off Portstewart this fine action shot illustrates the Coleraine Harbour pilot launch "Violet Clarke" at work in the bay. On board are boatman Willie Smyrl with pilot Clarence Doherty returning to harbour after leaving a ship outward bound from Coleraine. The boat was built by ex-servicemen in Coleraine following a drowning tragedy off Portstewart in January 1923 and remained in service for over 40 years.

Author's Collection

Cromore Station Trains actually stopped at Portstewart railway station, known as Cromore Halt, right up until the 1960s. Engine number 71 is seen here ready to depart, tender first, for Coleraine and beyond during the 1950s. Although trains to Portrush still pass through here the station building itself has been converted into private homes and many of the railway features such as platforms, footbridge, signal box and water tower have all been removed. "Cromore Halt" is now the name of a nearby hostelry.

Tommy McDonald Collection

Lansdowne Terrace A Dronthiem boat with a very early Coleraine fishing registration number (CE2) makes its way into Port-an-Dhu harbour at Lansdowne in Portrush in the early 1920s. In the background stands the famed Northern Counties Hotel with its gardens and nearby sea bath house.

Courtesy Jim Allen

Barry's Amusements No outing to "the Port" was complete without a visit to Barry's amusements. This lovely 1950s view of the outdoor attractions is sure to evoke many fond memories. The "Big Wheel", "Helter Skelter" and "Wee Train" were simple attractions by today's standards but loved by generations of children. In the background can be seen the main entrance to the indoor attractions as well as the magnificent Victorian station building dating from 1893.

Tommy McDonald Collection

Arcadia Site There are countless photographs existing of the Arcadia in a variety of guises. The earliest tea kiosk through to the large ballroom complex of the 1960s have all been the subject of postcards and photos over the years. This rare early picture illustrates the shoreline from the East Strand to the area known as the "Ladies' Bathing Place". Only bathing boxes exist at the water's edge with the large properties of Causeway Street visible in the background.

Diane Kirkpatrick Collection

Arcadia Ballroom An extremely popular venue during the 1950s and 1960s the Arcadia Ballroom regularly attracted hordes of young people at weekends to dances featuring the legendary Dave Glover Showband. This picture illustrates the location on a sunny afternoon during high summer season when the promenade, café and ice cream parlour were thronged with day trippers from all over the province.

Tommy McDonald Collection

Portrush Landmarks The Northern Counties Hotel and Fawcett's Royal Hotel feature prominently in this 1950s view of a seemingly deserted Portrush. Closer inspection of the picture however, reveals a few individuals on the streets in addition to a painter in white overalls next to his ladder at the front of the Northern Counties. The area of garden in front of the hotels has recently been the subject of intensive archaeological excavations which have revealed more of Portrush's ancient past.

Tommy McDonald Collection

S.S. LONSDALE This well attended scene was photographed on the West Strand in Portrush some days after the grounding of the unfortunate vessel shortly after leaving Portrush Harbour in November 1926. LONSDALE was to become quite a feature on the beach below Castle Erin for several months as various attempts were made to refloat her. This was eventually achieved in the spring of 1927 and the ship sailed away under her own steam. Few photos of the incident survive.

Diane Kirkpatrick Collection

Other Publications available from IMPACT

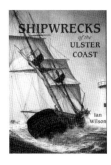
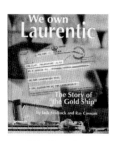